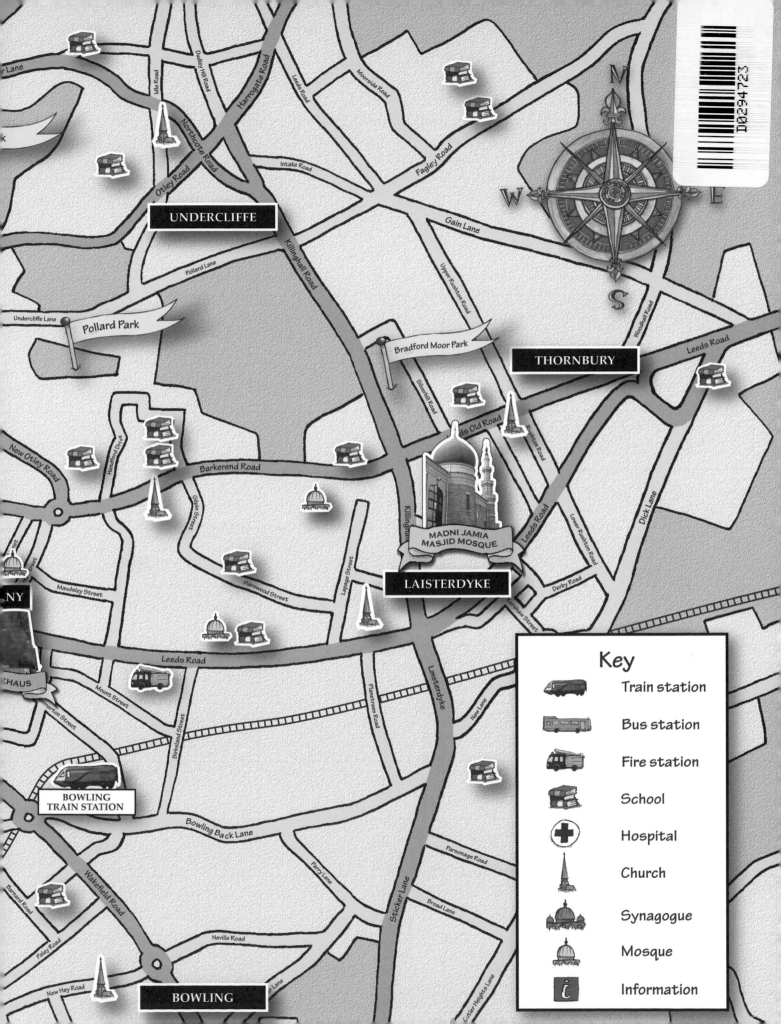

children's HISTORY of
BRADFORD

Written by
Maggie Wilson

HOMETOWN WORLD

How well do you know your town?

Have you ever wondered what it would have been like living in Bradford during Medieval times? What about becoming a mill worker in one of Bradford's Victorian woollen mills? This book will uncover the important and exciting things that happened in your town.

Want to hear the other good bits? Some fairly brainy folk have worked on this book to make sure it's fun and informative. So what are you waiting for? Peel back the pages and be amazed at the story behind your town.

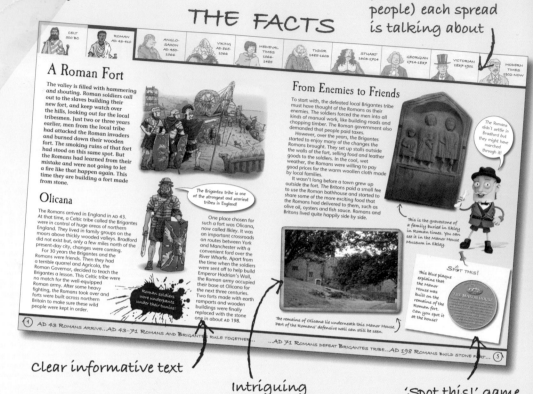

Timeline shows which period (dates and people) each spread is talking about

THE FACTS

Clear informative text

Intriguing old photos

'Spot this!' game with hints on something to find in your town

THE EVIDENCE

Go back in time to read what it was like for children growing up in Bradford.

Hometown facts to amaze you!

Each period in the book ends with a summary explaining how we know about the past.

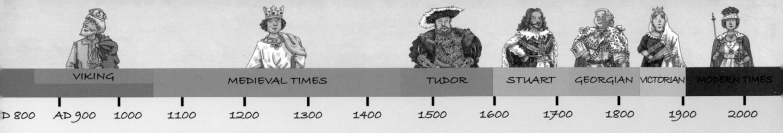

Contents

CELT
500 BC

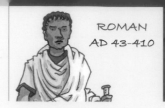
ROMAN
AD 43–410

ANGLO-
SAXON
AD 450–
1066

VIKING
AD 865–
1066

MEDIEV.
TIMES
1066–
1485

A Roman Fort

The valley is filled with hammering and shouting. Roman soldiers call out to the slaves building their new fort, and keep watch over the hills, looking out for the local tribesmen. Just two or three years earlier, men from the local tribe had attacked the Roman invaders and burned down their wooden fort. The smoking ruins of that fort had stood on this same spot. But the Romans had learned from their mistake and were not going to let a fire like that happen again. This time they are building a fort made from stone.

Olicana

The Romans arrived in England in AD 43. At that time, a Celtic tribe called the Brigantes were in control of huge areas of northern England. They lived in family groups on the moors above thickly wooded valleys. Bradford did not exist but, only a few miles north of the present-day city, changes were coming.

For 30 years the Brigantes and the Romans were friends. Then they had a terrible quarrel and Agricola, the Roman Governor, decided to teach the Brigantes a lesson. This Celtic tribe were no match for the well-equipped Roman army. After some heavy fighting, the Romans took over and forts were built across northern Britain to make sure these wild people were kept in order.

The Brigantes tribe is one of the strongest and scariest tribes in England!

One place chosen for such a fort was Olicana, now called Ilkley. It was an important crossroads on routes between York and Manchester with a convenient ford over the River Wharfe. Apart from the time when the soldiers were sent off to help build Emperor Hadrian's Wall, the Roman army occupied their base at Olicana for the next three centuries. Two forts made with earth ramparts and wooden buildings were finally replaced with the stone one in about AD 198.

Roman soldiers wore underpants under their tunics!

From Enemies to Friends

To start with, the defeated local Brigantes tribe must have thought of the Romans as their enemies. The soldiers forced the men into all kinds of manual work, like building roads and chopping timber. The Roman government also demanded that people paid taxes.

However, over the years, the Brigantes started to enjoy many of the changes the Romans brought. They set up stalls outside the walls of the fort, selling food and leather goods to the soldiers. In the cool, wet weather, the Romans were willing to pay good prices for the warm woollen cloth made by local families.

It wasn't long before a town grew up outside the fort. The Britons paid a small fee to use the Roman bathhouse and started to share some of the more exciting food that the Romans had delivered to them, such as olive oil, oysters and fish sauce. Romans and Britons lived quite happily side by side.

The Romans didn't settle in Bradford but they might have marched through it!

This is the gravestone of a family buried in Ilkley in Roman times. You can see it in the Manor House Museum in Ilkley.

The remains of Olicana lie underneath this Manor House. Part of the Romans' defensive wall can still be seen.

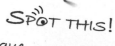 SPOT THIS!

This blue plaque explains that the Manor House was built on the remains of the Roman fort. Can you spot it at the house?

ILKLEY CIVIC SOCIETY

THE MANOR HOUSE
Originating in the 14th century and formerly known as The Castle, this mainly 17th century house was built on the remains of the Roman Fort. By 1804 it was divided into cottages. In 1955 it was saved from demolition when Percy Dalton donated it to the community. It was converted into the Art Gallery and Museum in 1961.

CELT
500 BC

ROMAN
AD 43-410

ANGLO-
SAXON
AD 450-
1066

VIKING
AD 865-
1066

MEDIEVA
TIMES
1066-
1485

A local boy was standing on the moor above Olicana, looking after his family's sheep and watching the Romans build their fort. He is an imaginary character called Godric. Here, Godric is daydreaming about his secret ambition. What would his grandfather have said about this?

Haven't you heard of abbacchio? It's a Roman recipe and the main ingredient is...lamb!

I would love to be a Roman soldier! Imagine wearing that red tunic, the leather belt, the breastplate and shiny metal helmet! I'd be the smartest soldier on parade and the best at carrying out the daily drill. I would march along the roads, keeping a lookout for any sign of trouble, and my hobnail boots would never slip. With my left arm looped through the back of my shield I'd be safe from anything. My right arm would be ready to grab my sword if I suddenly needed to defend myself from attack.

Back in the fort, I could be a sentry or learn how to make weapons in the iron works. Maybe I could help look after the horses occasionally, too. I might even learn Latin and work in the headquarters. I could write up the journal for the cohort or be in charge of the soldiers' pay.

I would have to join up for twenty-five years but when I finished I would get a piece of land or a good amount of money to start my own business. I would travel and see faraway places, like the massive fort at York that I've heard about. Life would be exciting and I would be important. I'd be proud to be part of the Roman army and I wouldn't have to waste my days watching stupid sheep...

Hobnailed boots have nails in the soles to give them grip and make them last longer.

TUDOR
1485-1603

STUART
1603-1714

GEORGIAN
1714-1837

VICTORIAN
1837-1901

MODERN
TIMES
1902-NOW

Plan of Fort at Olicana

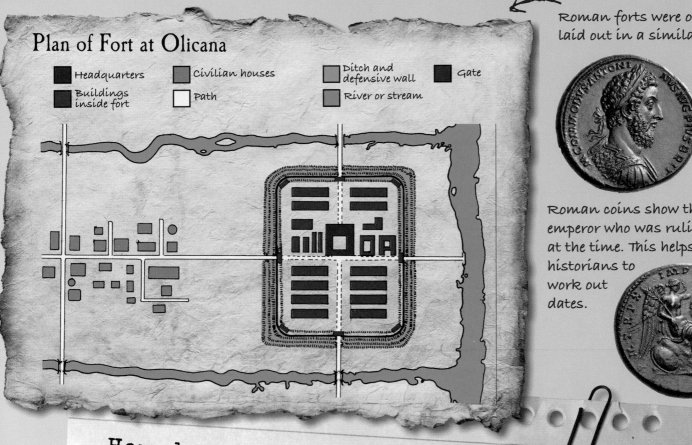

- ■ Headquarters
- ■ Buildings inside fort
- ■ Civilian houses
- □ Path
- ■ Ditch and defensive wall
- ■ River or stream
- ■ Gate

Roman forts were often laid out in a similar way.

Roman coins show the emperor who was ruling at the time. This helps historians to work out dates.

How do we know?

After the Romans left Olicana, their fort collapsed. Since then, archaeologists have found the ruins and can work out what the fort looked like. They also found Roman gravestones which tell us a bit about the people who lived there. Pictures carved onto the gravestones show the clothes people wore and even what hairstyles they had!

Letters written to soldiers on wooden tablets were found at a Roman fort on Hadrian's Wall. They tell us that the men were sent socks and warm underwear. The Roman army must have thought England was cold!

We know about food the Romans liked because archaeologists have found bones and oyster shells. Also, when cooking pots and jars are dug up, scientists can sometimes work out what they were filled with.

Norman Knights

William the Conqueror's gang of knights gallops through the wooded valley of Bradfordale, setting fire to cottages and fields and chasing after men, women and children. The villagers scream and run. Those who escape have to watch as the food they have been growing and storing for the coming year goes up in smoke. The people of Bradford will now face starvation. Will they survive?

A Small Village

After the Romans left England, other tribes of people continued to invade the country. The first invaders were the Jutes and Angles, from Denmark, followed by the Saxons from northern Germany. Later, the Vikings arrived. They were a German tribe who had settled in Scandinavia. They left little evidence in Bradford.

At this time, Bradford was only a very small village in Northumbria. People lived at the 'broad ford' near the Beck, and that is how the village got its name. Bradfordale was the name of the valley where three streams met to become Bradford Beck.

Destruction!

In 1066, William of Normandy won a great victory against the English at Hastings, in the south-east of England, and was crowned king. He became known as William the Conqueror. Yorkshiremen did not want a Frenchman as King of England so they attacked his castle in York. As a punishment for daring to challenge his power, William sent Ilbert de Lacy and an army of knights to Yorkshire to destroy the land and burn the towns and villages.

Map of Angle-Land

PICTLAND

STRATHCLYDE

Ad Murum (Newcastle)

Hadrian's Wall

NORTHUMBRIA

LINDSEY

EAST ANGLIA

MERCIA

ESSEX

HWICCA

KENT

WESSEX

SUSSEX

N

Bradford was in the Anglo-Saxon kingdom of Northumbria.

TUDOR
1485-1603

STUART
1603-1714

GEORGIAN
1714-1837

VICTORIAN
1837-1901

MODERN
TIMES
1902-
NOW

A Market Town

After William I's savage actions, only a handful of people were left in Bradford. But the village slowly recovered and, over the following centuries, Bradford grew into a busy little market town of about 650 people. The wooden church was rebuilt in stone, where it still stands on the hill above the city centre today. The Manor Hall, where the Lords' stewards collected rents, was where Hall Ings is and there were three muddy narrow streets – Kirkgate, Ivegate and Westgate.

In 1251, Bradford was given a charter, which meant the village could hold a market every Thursday. Shoppers could buy woollen cloth that had been woven in the stallholder's home, or leather goods made in local workshops.

In 1277, Bradford was first officially described as a town, with a market place, a gallows and an early type of town court.

> 'Gate' was the Old English word for 'street'.

> Wormwood, comfrey and vinegar - that should cure you!

Troubled Times

But Bradford's troubles were not over. In 1314, the Scots raided English towns and villages. People in Bradford were killed and the church was nearly destroyed. Then, for several summers in a row, the weather was bad and harvests were ruined. Once again, Bradford people were starving. Children were told to stay inside because if they played outside they might be grabbed and eaten!

> In medieval times, Bradford changed from a tiny village into a busy market town.

> ᗐ
> **SPOT THIS!**
>
> There is part of an Anglo-Saxon cross in Bradford Cathedral. Look carefully along the north wall to try and spot it.

The Black Death

As if that wasn't enough, the Black Death then hit the town. The Black Death was a type of plague carried by fleas on rats. Many people in Bradford caught the plague and came out in a rash, followed by black lumps the size of onions. These lumps burst, oozing foul pus. Most victims died quickly after that.

By the end of the 14th century, there were only about half as many people in Bradford as there had been 150 years before. But once again the brave little town survived.

CELT
500 BC

ROMAN
AD 43-410

ANGLO-
SAXON
AD 450-
1066

VIKING
AD 865-
1066

MEDIEVA
TIMES
1066-148

Ten year-old Martha lives in Bradford in 1357. Her father works in the wool industry, which is starting to do very well in Bradford. In this imaginary account, Martha tells us about crime and punishment.

Ducking was a form of punishment often used for women suspected to be witches. The victim was strapped to a chair and plunged into water.

Yesterday, I threw a rotten egg at Richard the tanner! He was locked in the pillory after dumping waste from his business into the Bradford Beck. The water was not fast enough to wash away the rotting remains, scraped from animal skins. The hue and cry had been raised to catch Richard and he was soon caught. He was taken to the Manor Court for punishment to be decided, and then ended up in the pillory.

I was in the crowd at the court today because my brother, Jacob, punched someone when he was drunk. After a night in the prison, Jacob was taken to face the steward. He had to pay a heavy fine – three shillings and fourpence.

I thought a better punishment to cool his temper would have been a ducking in the Beck but my family laughed at the suggestion. Apparently only women are punished by ducking.

I remember when my neighbour, Mistress Meg, was accused of being a gossip and spreading rumours. She was dragged to the ducking stool and strapped to it, then lowered completely into the water twice. It was a cold day and she caught a terrible chill. Criminals don't get away with much in our town – the worst are hanged on the gallows!

A hue and cry is when everyone is called out to catch a criminal, like Richard over there!

Urgh! Rotten fruit stinks but rotten eggs are the worst!

❧ REWARD! ❧

BEWARE the Bradford Boar! This wild beast lives in Cliffe Wood and has frightened many good townsfolk.

Could YOU be the one to slay this fierce beast?

To claim your reward, chop off the boar's head and deliver it to Manor Court.

The Bradford Boar

According to a medieval legend, a huge wild boar lived in Cliffe Wood, near Bradford, frightening the people. A reward was offered for killing the boar.

One day, a huntsman, who we think was called John Northrup, saw the boar and shot it with his bow and arrow. The boar's head was heavy so John cut out the tongue as evidence that he had killed the animal. Then he set off for court.

Soon afterwards, another man found the dead boar. He cut off its head and rushed to claim the reward. He got to the court first but couldn't explain why the boar's head had no tongue. When John turned up with the tongue, it proved he was the real hero. That's why Bradford's Coat of Arms has a boar's head with no tongue!

PROGRESS·INDUSTRY·HUMANITY

How do we know?

We know about William I's destruction of Yorkshire from the Domesday Book – his record of how much land people owned. Written in 1086, the Domesday Book says that Bradford belonged to Ilbert de Lacey but describes it as 'waste' land.

We know there was a ducking stool and gallows in Bradford because they are marked on old maps of the town. Records from the manor court mention a tanner in 1357 who, like Richard, was punished for sweeping his waste into the Beck.

Roadnames in Bradford also give us clues about the past. We know that 'Ings' meant 'meadow', so Hall Ings was once land where the lord of the manor allowed his animals to graze. Old documents also mention Kirkgate, Westgate and Ivegate. We know where the old prison was because there is still a cell under the road at the top of Ivegate!

Now you know the story behind the boar's head on Bradford's Coat of Arms!

CELT
500 BC

ROMAN
AD 43-410

ANGLO-
SAXON
AD 450-
1066

VIKING
AD 865-
1066

MEDIEV
TIMES
1066-
1485

Good Times at Last

It is late afternoon on a warm summer's day. A group of boys are clattering cheerfully down Ivegate towards the Bradford Beck. They are the sons of tradesmen who have done well in Bradford in the last few years, making leather and trading woollen cloth.

The boys have been studying Latin and mathematics all day at the Grammar School and they are happy to be free for an hour or so. They're going to the Beck for a swim and a splash around to cool down. Then they will head for home, hungry for their evening meal.

Tudor Bradford

During Tudor times, Bradford was recovering from the troubles of the Middle Ages and was starting to become a successful town. There was a new class of men in Bradford who were doing well in trading woollen cloth and leather items such as shoes. Some had their own tanning works to make the leather.

Most of the wool trade was run by merchants, who often grew rich from the profits. The tradesmen and their families lived in large houses on Westgate which were two storeys high and built of stone. They could afford to send their sons to the local Grammar School, which opened in 1548 as a result of Henry VIII destroying local monasteries.

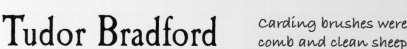
Carding brushes were used to comb and clean sheep's wool.

A New Religion

Religion was very important in Tudor times. In order to divorce his first wife, Henry VIII decided to separate England from the Catholic church. The king ordered abbeys and monasteries throughout England to be destroyed, including Kirkstall Abbey, Bolton Abbey and Fountains Abbey. He then made himself the head of the new Church of England. This caused many religious arguments across the country.

Elizabeth I later tried to settle the arguments her father had begun. She also ordered a new Bible to be written in English. Most people in Bradford were happy living under Elizabeth I's rule.

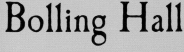

Bolling Hall

The parish church in Bradford was a fine stone building with a tower – the same one that you can still see today. The inside of the church was plain, as Bradford worshippers liked it, without statues and decorations to distract them from praying.

Not everyone in Bradford agreed with the new religious ways. The Tempest family – an important family who lived in Bolling Hall – were still Catholics. They liked the Latin Bible and thought that having a plain church was disrespectful to God. Sir Nicholas Tempest had been very angry when King Henry VIII ordered the abbeys to be destroyed. He joined a march in protest to the king and ended up in prison. Even Queen Elizabeth could not force the Tempests to attend the Parish Church, so they paid a fine every week instead.

Overall, Tudor times were good times for Bradford and John Leland, a visitor to the town, described Bradford as 'a pretty, quick Market Towne'.

Bolling Hall was home to the Tempest family.

The imaginary account below is from Jane – a young girl who cards wool for her mother.

A spinning wheel cost around one shilling and ten pence in Tudor times – about a day's wages for many families.

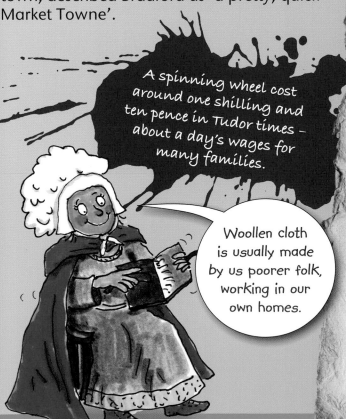

Woollen cloth is usually made by us poorer folk, working in our own homes.

Every week, a wool merchant comes round with bundles of sheep's wool, still mucky from the sheep. My job is to card the wool. That means combing it with special, sharp brushes to get all the dirt and tangles out. After it's cleaned, my mother uses her spinning wheel to twist the short strands into yarn. The merchant takes the yarn to one of our neighbours, who weaves it into cloth. The woollen cloth is sold in the market or perhaps used to make cushions. Bradford is famous for making cushions, you know.

Of course, I have plenty of other things to do like feeding the chickens, collecting water and emptying the chamber pot. I get tired sometimes but I don't have time to be bored! I'd love to go to school but girls aren't allowed to and anyway, my family couldn't afford it.

Down with King Charles!

A young Bradford man crouching at the top of the church tower has just fired his musket, shooting the soldier in charge of the Royalist cannon. That was the signal for the rest of Bradford's defenders to charge up the bank and take on their Royalist enemies using swords, pitchforks and other farm tools. The men of Bradford may not have the best weapons and armour but they are proud of their town and are determined not to let the king's army win.

Most people in Bradford supported parliament in the English Civil Wars. They didn't want a king and were nicknamed Roundheads because of their short hairstyles.

Civil War

By 1600, Bradford was thriving, with a population of about 2,500 people. But new troubles were about to begin.

In 1642, King Charles I of England declared war against his own parliament, and the fighting that followed is called the English Civil Wars. Bradford people had come to hate King Charles. He had not treated the town well and had demanded new, unfair taxes. He had tried to stop the Puritan style of religion that Bradford people liked and allowed the Tempest family to hand out harsh punishments in the local court. By the time the war started, there was no doubt which side Bradford would support. Some of the younger men went to join Parliament's army and those left behind prepared to defend the town from Royalist attacks.

TUDOR
1485-1603

STUART
1603-1714

GEORGIAN
1714-1837

VICTORIAN
1837-1901

MODERN
TIMES
1902-NOW

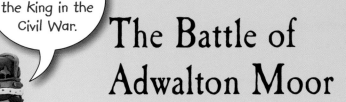

Bradford fought against the King in the Civil War.

The First Attacks

Bradford was attacked for the first time in October 1642, when 300 local men took on more than 700 Royalist soldiers. They had prepared well, using sacks of wool to protect the church tower, which was the best look-out point for miles around. But before any damage was done, one of the Royalist cannons suddenly exploded by itself and then a terrible snow storm drove the attackers back to Leeds. Bradford remained strong.

On 18th December 1642, the Duke of Newcastle sent troops from the King's Royalist army in Leeds to attack Bradford for the second time. It was a Sunday morning and the Duke hoped to surprise the town while everyone was at church. But spies had warned the people in Bradford about the Duke's plans. The brave men of Bradford charged forward to fight the Royalists, and forced them to retreat.

The Battle of Adwalton Moor

The Duke of Newcastle was determined to punish Bradford once and for all. In 1643, he took his army to Adwalton Moor, near Bradford, and a tremendous battle took place. This time, the Royalists won. The wool sacks on the church tower were shot down. Women and children ran into their houses, frightened and crying. The Duke of Newcastle went to spend the night at Bolling Hall with his friends, the Tempests. Bradford's soldiers had been defeated.

SPOT THIS!

If you visit the site of the Battle of Adwalton Moor, look out for this memorial stone.

The End of the Wars

The Roundheads eventually won the Civil War overall. King Charles was put on trial and then executed. Despite supporting the winning side in the end, Bradford had suffered in the fighting. A serious attack of plague in 1666 meant Bradford took a long time to recover its fortunes.

Charles I had his head chopped off in 1649. For 11 years, England had no king or queen!

CELT
500 BC

ROMAN
AD 43-410

ANGLO-
SAXON
AD 450-
1066

VIKING
AD 865-
1066

MEDIEV
TIMES
1066
1485

Thomas is an imaginary character living in Bradford during the Civil War. In this letter to his friend, Thomas talks about the battle he saw on Adwalton Moor.

I wish I was old enough to fight for Lord Fairfax.

Guess what? Yesterday I followed Lord Fairfax as he led our army out of Bradford, and I saw a battle on Adwalton Moor. A real battle! I wish I was fourteen – then I'd be allowed to fight too.

From my hiding place in the wood, I saw the two armies line up, facing each other across the moor. The cavalry were round the sides and behind the soldiers on foot. The Royalists had thousands more men than us but we were brave and determined.

Suddenly the battle started. You can't imagine the noise – galloping hooves, gunfire, clashing swords, shouting and screaming. As horses charged, men were knocked to the ground. An arm that had been hacked off by a sword landed on the grass in front of me!

Our soldiers were defending themselves behind hedges and, when the Royalist horsemen tried to get through the gaps, they were blasted back by musket fire. Then our men came out into the middle of the moor to finish off the Royalist infantry.

The Duke of Newcastle was about to surrender when his pikemen decided to make one last charge. Lots of our troops were killed – I saw one man with a pike going right through him! We were outnumbered and had to retreat. What will happen to Bradford now?

Lord Fairfax led the Roundheads in battles across Yorkshire.

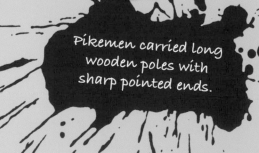

Pikemen carried long wooden poles with sharp pointed ends.

TUDOR
1485-1603

STUART
1603-1714

GEORGIAN
1714-1837

VICTORIAN
1837-1901

MODERN
TIMES
1902-NOW

The Ghost of Bolling Hall

The Duke of Newcastle was very pleased with the great battle he had won in 1643. He hoped for a good night's sleep in his room in Bolling Hall. The next day he planned to send his army into Bradford to take anything they wanted from the townsfolk. The soldiers would be allowed to rampage through the streets, destroying homes and killing men, women and children.

But while he was sleeping, the Duke was disturbed by a ghostly white figure pulling at his bedclothes and crying 'Pity poor Bradford! Pity poor Bradford!' This figure has become known as the ghost of Bolling Hall.

In the morning the Royalists did go and rob goods from the houses but the people were not murdered. Had the ghost persuaded the Duke not to be too cruel?

How do we know?

Archaeologists have explored Adwalton Moor and have found lots of musket-balls and cannon-balls, so we know where the battlefield was. Some people still pick up bits and pieces from the fighting as they walk around the area. We know about the details of the battle because Sir Thomas Fairfax, who was one of the Parliamentary army leaders, wrote about it in his memoirs.

A 15 year-old boy called Joseph Lister was involved in the Siege of Bradford and he wrote down what he saw in great detail in his book 'A Genuine Account'. He explains how frightened people were during the civil wars.

Bolling Hall is now a museum. Armour and weaponry found from that time are on display and the rooms are set out so we can imagine what the house was like when the Tempests lived there.

The Duke of Newcastle was sleeping in this room in Bolling Hall when the 'ghost' appeared!

Changing Times

In the middle of the pushing crowd, an old man holds on tightly to his grandson's hand. He is nearly as excited as the little boy! They will soon have their first sight of a steam train, as it puffs into Bradford's brand new railway station at the end of Market Street. The day has been declared a public holiday and even though the train is very late, it seems most of Bradford has come to watch it arrive.

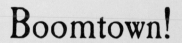

In Georgian times, horses pulled narrowboats along canals, like this.

If the canal in Bradford is re-opened, it will be the only canal ever to be closed twice and re-opened twice!

Boomtown!

The Industrial Revolution began in Britain in the 1760s. There were huge improvements in machinery, transport and technology which turned industrial towns like Bradford into 'boomtowns'. Bradford grew massively during this time and became known as the 'wool capital of the world'.

In 1774, a canal was completed beside the Beck with flat-bottomed boats dragged along by huge horses. It became a busy waterway with barges full of coal from the mines. The canal quickly became polluted.

In 1846, Bradford's first train station was opened at the end of Market Street. Crowds gathered in excitement to see a steam train chug into Bradford. Travelling by railway was even faster than by canal so tradesmen and industries soon started using trains to transport goods instead.

...1760s INDUSTRIAL REVOLUTION BEGINS...1774 BRADFORD'S CANAL OPENS...

Growing Fast

In 1801, there was only one mill in Bradford. But by 1841 there were 67 mills and by 1850 there were more than 103,000 people living in the town. Bradford was growing faster than any other town in England!

New narrow roads of back-to-back houses were built, such as the well-known Gaythorne Street in Great Horton. Off the old main streets there were dark, dirty alleys, crowded with higgledy-piggledy housing. There were no proper drains at this time so all sewage and waste ran down the streets into Bradford Beck. The water in the Beck was brown and sludgy, with bubbles of smelly gas erupting every now and again from below the surface. The smell would have been disgusting!

During this time a group of German wool merchants moved to Bradford and increased trade by setting up large warehouses. The area where they lived and worked is still called Little Germany.

> Bradford was the fastest-growing town in England in the early 1800s!

Lister's Mill is a famous part of Bradford's skyline. It was the biggest silk factory in the world!

Dirt and Danger

Bradford mill owners were becoming rich and important. They had helped to pay for the canal, for improved roads to other towns and for the railway. They bought machines made at the ironworks in Low Moor. They built mills and housing for their workers.

But some of these men were worried. Clouds of smoke from all the chimneys hung over the crowded town centre. Many of the roads were covered in mud and slime. After dark, it was dangerous to walk about because of drunkenness and fighting. Bradford was described as 'the most filthy town' in the north.

Lots more changes needed to be made before Bradfordians could really feel proud.

SPOT THIS!

Grandad's chair and clock are in the Little Germany area of Bradford. The sculpture, carved from sandstone, was designed to represent a mill owner's office.

Monstrous Mills

It is 6 o'clock in the morning and the children in the mill have just started work. Sunlight struggles to shine in through the dirty windows, showing streams of dust in the air. The spinning machines whirr and clatter. The children won't finish work until 7 or 8 o'clock at night, sorting bobbins and picking up loose cotton from the floor. If they don't work hard enough, the overlooker beats them with a leather strap!

Children Needed!

Whole families, including children as young as 4 years old, were set to work in the mills. Only children were small enough to do some of the jobs, like crawling under the machines to clear out the fluff. Also, children could be paid much less than adults so they were cheap for mill owners to employ.

Sometimes the overlooker twists our ears to wake us up!

New Inventions

Clever inventors had produced machines that could spin many times more yarn than one person could with a spinning wheel. Each new invention seemed to lead to another one that was bigger and faster. None of the machines would fit into an ordinary room so mills were built where rows of steam-powered spinning frames could be lined up side by side.

There are lots of different spinning machines on display at Bradford's Industrial Museum.

...1853 MILL IN SALTAIRE IS COMPLETED...1873 LISTER'S MILL IS BUILT...

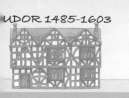

Accidents Happened

The mills were usually large and had plenty of space. But the steam from the machinery made the air very hot, stuffy and full of dust. Workers were not allowed to open the windows because that could harm the wool. The machines were extremely noisy and there were no rails to protect children from getting caught in the moving parts. One factory inspector described an accident when a girl got her apron trapped. She was twirled round in between parts of the machine and her leg was cut off.

Bradford became a city during Victorian times. It was bursting with mill workers!

Titus Salt was one of Bradford's better mill owners. He became mayor of Bradford in 1848.

Good Mill Owners

Some mill owners were more caring and did what they could to make conditions better for their workers. The most famous mill owners in Bradford were John Wood and Titus Salt. John Wood helped make working conditions better for children and paid to have a doctor in his mill, to make sure his workers were healthy.

Titus Salt could see that Bradford had become very polluted with smoke from all the chimneys, and that the houses were dirty and overcrowded. Disease spread quickly, and far too many people died young. He realised that people in his mills would work better if they were healthy.

Salt decided to move his mill to the countryside about four miles outside Bradford, and built Saltaire village beside the mill for his workers to live in. The brand new village had two churches, schools, a library, a hospital, almshouses, a public baths and a social club. Pubs weren't allowed!

SPOT THIS!

This is the gravestone of some orphans who worked in the factory at Wainstalls, near Bradford.

Hannah is a girl who might have lived in Saltaire in about 1868. In this imagined account she explains how Titus Salt changed her life.

The new houses in Saltaire would have been very appealing to poor families like Hannah's.

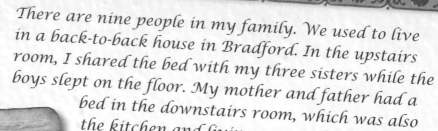

There are nine people in my family. We used to live in a back-to-back house in Bradford. In the upstairs room, I shared the bed with my three sisters while the boys slept on the floor. My mother and father had a bed in the downstairs room, which was also the kitchen and living room. Oh, and the baby slept in the bottom drawer of a chest!

The chimney from the fireplace was terribly smoky. Worst of all was the toilet. We had to share an outside privy with five other families. It was in a yard at the back of the row of houses and it was always overflowing. The smell was horrible!

It was a very lucky day when my family went to work at Sir Titus Salt's new mill. We moved to Saltaire to live and it was like we'd gone to heaven! Work in the mill is still hard but the village is perfect. The streets are wide and clean and there is a park down the road with a bandstand and a cricket pitch.

Our new house is wonderful. It has two proper bedrooms and one room downstairs with a scullery at the back. We have gas lights and fresh water that comes through a pipe to a tap right inside our house. Best of all, our house has a small yard and our very own outside toilet.

I work in the mill but I'm called a half-timer because I go to school as well. In Saltaire there is a school for boys but there's one for girls too. We learn how to read and write and do arithmetic.

Poo-ey! Having our own privy doesn't mean it smells any better!

22

A statue of Titus Salt looks over Roberts Park in Saltaire.

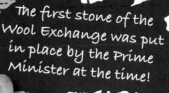

The first stone of the Wool Exchange was put in place by the Prime Minister at the time!

The Wool Exchange was built between 1864 and 1867 as a place for wool traders to meet.

A steam engine at the Industrial Museum

How do we know?

We know what the mill buildings were like because there are still many left in Bradford, though most are not used for making cloth any more. We can see steam engines and the old spinning and weaving machines in Bradford's Industrial Museum. Sometimes there are demonstrations, showing how they worked and how noisy they were!

There are no photographs of the first steam train in Bradford or of the overcrowded houses and dirty streets, but there are some paintings and drawings which help us to understand what the town was like. We can also find out lots about Bradford from reports that were written to explain how smelly and filthy conditions were, trying to persuade the town council to make improvements.

CELT
500 BC

ROMAN
AD 43-410

ANGLO-
SAXON
AD 450-
1066

VIKING
AD 865-
1066

MEDIEV
TIMES
1066-
1485

An Exhibition

The sun is shining and everyone in Bradford is out on the streets. Brightly-coloured bunting flutters between the lamp posts and band music fills the air. Soon the Prince and Princess of Wales will drive along Manningham Lane to open the Bradford Exhibition. This will show that Bradford's textiles are still among the best in the world. There are lots of exciting events and attractions for everyone – the men might visit the main hall to see the inventions and achievements of Bradford's industries; the ladies will flock to the Dress Show; the children will wait impatiently for their turn on the water chute.

A Grand City

In May 1904, an exhibition was opened at Cartwright Hall in Bradford's Lister Park. The main hall was filled with a huge display of inventions and creations from the city's textile industry. There were fashion shows for the ladies and entertainment for the children, including a water chute by the lake. Underneath the chute were about 20 small shops selling souvenirs. A large concert hall was also built, holding performances from local musicians including organists and singers.

Visitors would have come from all over the city and further afield to see the great inventions on display at Cartwright Hall in 1904.

...1904 CARTWRIGHT HALL IS OPENED AND BRADFORD EXHIBITION TAKES PLACE...

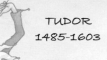 
Lots of new people came to Bradford in the 20th century, making it a very interesting place to live.

Newcomers!

Bradford is an exciting city, where people from all over the world can live side by side, sharing their ideas, their skills and their food! Bradford has benefited from many newcomers to the town, including Irish people, Italians, and many from Eastern Europe who lost their homes in World War Two.

In the 1950s, industries were beginning to grow again after all the hardships of the war. There were not enough people in Britain to fill all the jobs, so the British government sent out posters asking people in the West Indies, India and Pakistan to come and help. Men from Pakistan and India came to Bradford to work in the mills. Many began to miss their families and asked their wives and children to join them in England.

 SPOT THIS!

This statue of Queen Victoria was unveiled in 1904 on the first day of the Bradford Exhibition. Look out for it in a park between Morley Street and Little Horton Lane.

Into the Future

Since the 1960s, Bradford's Asian population has grown considerably. Asian shops and businesses are a very important part of the city. Children in schools learn about each other's religions and cultures. Bradford's Asian restaurants are famous all over England for their curries and other Asian specialities. There has been an Asian Lord Mayor of Bradford.

There have also been bad times when there were fights and riots in the streets. But in most parts of the city people of many different racial backgrounds mix and work well together, hoping to make Bradford into a truly happy, multicultural community.

This photograph was taken in Bradford in 1950. Many Asian families had portraits like this taken so they could send the photo to family in their homeland.

Some of the people who came to Bradford recorded their experiences. The imaginary story below comes from a Pakistani man called Timur who grew up in Bradford.

My name is Timur and I arrived in Bradford in 1955. I was eight years old. My father was here for nearly a year before my mother told me we were going to move to live with him. I was very sad to leave my old home but excited as well.

It took a long time for us to get to England. My father met us when we arrived, which was good because everything else seemed so strange. Nearly everyone I could see was white and I couldn't understand a word they said.

At first, we shared a house with another family. It was quite hard to find a place of our own because some landlords said they would not rent to 'coloureds'. That was what they called people who weren't white, as if all Pakistanis and Indians were the same. At last we moved into our own little terraced house. It was a happy street with a mixture of white families and newcomers. I soon found out that not everyone was racist.

I went to school and started to learn English. I worked hard because I wanted to be a doctor when I grew up. One of my new friends laughed when I told him that. He said that Pakistanis had no chance of getting that kind of job because they were expected to work in the mills. He may have been right then but things have changed since the 1950s. Today my son is a surgeon at Bradford Royal Infirmary!

When we first arrived here, I didn't speak any English at all!

This Asian man is working in a Bradford textile mill in the 1980s.

TUDOR
1485-1603

STUART
1603-1714

GEORGIAN
1714-1837

VICTORIAN
1837-1901

MODERN
TIMES
1902-NOW

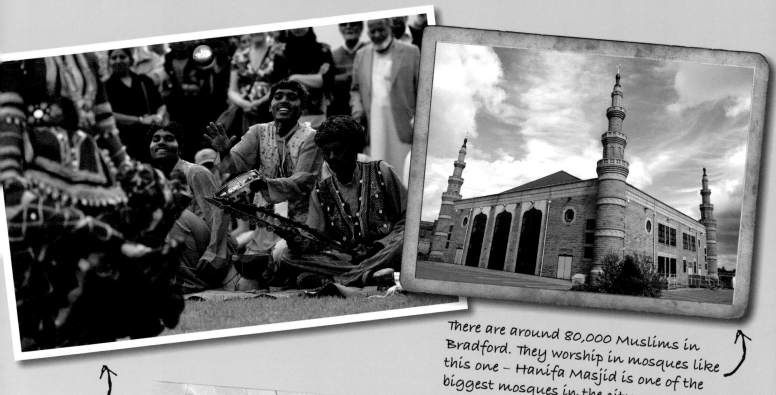

There are around 80,000 Muslims in Bradford. They worship in mosques like this one – Hanifa Masjid is one of the biggest mosques in the city.

The Mela takes place every year and is a fantastic celebration of music, dance and entertainment from Asian and other Bradford communities.

How do we know?

By 1904, cameras were regularly used to take pictures of important people, places and events. There are lots of photographs of the Bradford Exhibition and the Prince and Princess when they were in the city. Other photographs show us the streets of the city centre and the new electric trams. You can climb onto some of the originals in the Bradford Industrial Museum.

The best way to find out about what it was like to come to Bradford is to speak to people, and in the 1980s the Bradford Heritage Recording Unit did just that. They collected accounts from lots of people who came to Bradford in the 1950s, '60s and '70s. They made a tape recording and wrote a book called 'Destination Bradford'.

CELT
500 BC

ROMAN
AD 43-410

ANGLO-
SAXON
AD 450-
1066

VIKING
AD 865-
1066

MEDIEVA
TIME
1066
1485

Bradford Today and Tomorrow...

Bradford grew from a town into a city because of its successful textile mills. It has become known as a multicultural city, famous for award-winning films, David Hockney's paintings and the Brontë sisters' novels. The important thing to remember is that Bradford's history is about the people who lived through difficult or exciting or dangerous times – people like Godric, Martha, Thomas, Hannah and Timur!

City Square now has an open area with a mosaic called 'Bradford-on-sea'. How else could the city centre change over the next few years?

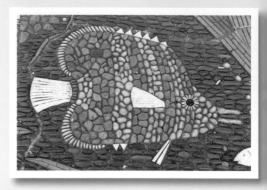

In 1983 the National Media Museum was opened. Will our mobile phones and computers be on display there one day for children of the future to laugh at?

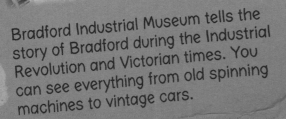

Bradford Industrial Museum tells the story of Bradford during the Industrial Revolution and Victorian times. You can see everything from old spinning machines to vintage cars.

The Needle is an example of modern sculpture in Bradford. It's 4.5 metres tall!

In 2009, Bradford became the world's first ever city of film!

BRADFORD
CITY OF FILM

...1937 FAMOUS ARTIST DAVID HOCKNEY IS BORN IN BRADFORD...

The old Odeon cinema

 SPOT THIS!

The Ivegate Arch includes scenes and icons from Bradford's past. Can you spot this one?

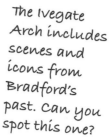

Some old buildings disappear from Bradford's landscape while new ones appear, like the Gatehaus.

You should feel proud to be a part of Bradford's future!

Have you ever watched a Bradford Bulls match?

In 1985, there was a terrible fire in Valley Parade Stadium. Memorials at the football ground today are a reminder of the tragedy.

The Alhambra Theatre shows ballets, operas and musicals. You can even have a party there!

How will they know?

How will future generations know what Bradford was like today? The Internet is a great way of recording what Bradford is like. Photos, blogs and stories from visitors can all spread the word about our wonderful Bradford. Museums like the Media Museum will also provide important evidence of how we live, for people in the future to see.

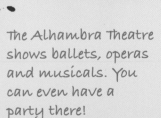

...1970 'THE RAILWAY CHILDREN' IS FILMED NEAR BRADFORD...

Glossary

Abbey – a building where monks or nuns live and work.

AD – a short way of writing the Latin words anno Domini, which mean 'in the year of our Lord', i.e. after the birth of Christ.

Archaeologist – a person who studies the past by examining buildings and objects left behind by previous people and cultures.

Bobbin – a small round device used for holding thread.

Breastplate – a piece of armour that protected a soldier's chest.

Bunting – colourful flags or streamers.

Catholic Church – also called the Roman Catholic Church: a Christian religion that is headed by the Pope.

Chamber pot – before toilets, people used chamber pots for going to the loo. They then had to empty them somewhere. Some people just threw the contents out the window.

Charter – written permission to do something. A Royal Charter means the King or Queen has given permission.

Church of England – a Christian religion that is headed by the king or queen.

Civil war – a war where people from the same country fight each other.

Cohort – a group of soldiers in the Roman Legion.

Domesday Book – William the Conqueror sent his men all over England to check how much land and wealth there was in the kingdom, and who owned it. The results were written in the Domesday Book.

Ford – a natural place to cross a river, where it's shallow.

Fort or fortress – a large, strong building offering support and protection.

Gallows – where people were hanged for crimes.

Hadrian's Wall – a wall that the Roman Emperor Hadrian ordered to be built across northern England to keep out the north British tribes.

Monastery – a place where monks live and worship.

Musket – a long-barrelled gun, loaded from the front, which was used from the 16th to the 18th century.

Overlooker – the person in charge, usually of a factory. Also called an overseer.

Parliamentarian – anyone who fought on the side of Oliver Cromwell and Parliament in the English Civil War. Sometimes they were called 'Roundheads' because of their short haircuts.

Plague – a disease that spreads easily and can kill.

Puritan – someone with very strict religious and moral rules.

Royalist – anyone who fought on the side of King Charles I in the English Civil War. Also known as a Cavalier.

Scullery – the part of a kitchen where vegetables were prepared and dishes washed. A scullery maid was one of the lowest servants in a household.

Sentry – someone who guards a place and looks out for danger.

Slave – any person who is owned by another. Slaves have no freedom or rights and work for no payment.

Tanner – a person who works with animal skins and 'tans' them, i.e. treats them so they can be turned into goods such as shoes and bags.

Index

...2009 BRADFORD BECOMES THE WORLD'S FIRST EVER CITY OF FILM...

31

Acknowledgements

The author and publishers would like to thank the following people:
Heather Millard from Bradford Museums and Galleries for her generous help in supplying us with fantastic images;
Bradford Industrial Museum and Bradford Cathedral for kindly allowing photography.

The publishers would like to thank the following people and organizations
for their permission to reproduce material on the following pages:
p5: Bradford Museums and Galleries; p6: www.saddlersden.co.uk; p7: Numismatica Ars Classica NAC AG, Zurich;
p10: Ihcoyc at en.wikipedia; p12: Paul Felix Photography/Alamy; p13: Bradford Museums and Galleries;
p14: 19th era/Alamy; p17: Bradford Museums and Galleries; p18: Duncan Davis/Alamy;
p20: Bradford Industrial Museum; p22: World History Archive/Alamy; p23: Bradford Industrial Museum;
p25: Photographer Tony Walker, copyright – Bradford Museums and Galleries; p26: mirpur 025_08a-Photographer
Tim Smith, copyright – Bradford Museums and Galleries; p27: Bradford Mela; p28: Bradford Industrial Museum,
Bradford City of Film Limited; p29: Bradford Bulls Holdings Limited.

All other images copyright of Hometown World

Written by Maggie Wilson
Educational consultant: Neil Thompson
Local history consultants: Local Studies team at Bradford Central Library
Designed by Stephen Prosser

Illustrated by Kate Davies, Mike Hall, Tim Hutchinson, Peter Kent,
John MacGregor, Leighton Noyes, Tim Sutcliffe and Dynamo Ltd
Additional photographs by Alex Long

First published by HOMETOWN WORLD in 2010
Hometown World Ltd
7 Northumberland Buildings
Bath BA1 2JB

www.hometownworld.co.uk

hb ISBN 978-1-84993-074-1
pb ISBN 978-1-84993-145-8

Your past
Your now
Your future

Your history4ever

Mmm...
Still love
chocolate
pudding!

My next one's going to
have 2 wheels!

Trophy for
the trendiest
glasses?

I love you too!